THE ULTIMATE

CROCKPOT

COOKBOOK

Irresistible Crockpot Recipes for Effortless Meals

BILL C. SHORT

TABLE OF CONTENT

CHAPTER 1

BREAKFAST DELIGHTS

CRISPY FRENCH TOAST STICKS

> ➢ *Serving Size: 4 servings*

> ➢ *Prep Time: 10 minutes*

> ➢ *Cooking Time: 10 minutes*

Nutrition Info (per serving):

- Calories: 250
- Total Fat: 10g
- Saturated Fat: 3g
- Cholesterol: 100mg
- Sodium: 350mg
- Total Carbohydrates: 30g
- Dietary Fiber: 2g
- Sugars: 8g
- Protein: 10g

Ingredients:

- 8 slices of bread (white or whole wheat)
- 2 large eggs

- 1/2 cup milk
- 1 teaspoon vanilla extract
- 1/2 teaspoon ground cinnamon
- 1/4 teaspoon ground nutmeg
- 1/4 teaspoon salt
- 1 cup cornflakes, crushed
- 2 tablespoons butter, melted
- Maple syrup, for serving

Directions:

1. Preheat your oven to 375°F (190°C) and line a baking sheet with parchment paper.

2. Cut each slice of bread into three strips to form sticks.

3. In a shallow dish, whisk together the eggs, milk, vanilla extract, cinnamon, nutmeg, and salt.

4. In another shallow dish, combine the crushed cornflakes with the melted butter.

5. Dip each bread stick into the egg mixture, allowing excess to drip off, then coat evenly with the cornflake mixture.

6. Place the coated sticks on the prepared baking sheet.

7. Bake for 10-12 minutes, flipping halfway through, until golden brown and crispy.

8. Serve hot with maple syrup for dipping.

AIR-FRIED BREAKFAST BURRITOS

> ➢ *Serving Size: 4 burritos*

> ➢ *Cooking Time: 15 minutes*

> ➢ *Prep Time: 10 minutes*

Nutrition Info (per burrito):

- Calories: 320
- Total Fat: 18g
- Saturated Fat: 7g
- Cholesterol: 220mg
- Sodium: 620mg
- Total Carbohydrates: 20g
- Dietary Fiber: 2g
- Sugars: 2g
- Protein: 20g

Ingredients:

- 4 large flour tortillas
- 8 large eggs
- 1/4 cup milk
- 1 cup shredded cheddar cheese

- 1 cup cooked and crumbled breakfast sausage
- 1/2 cup diced bell peppers
- 1/4 cup diced onions
- Salt and pepper to taste
- Cooking spray

Directions:

1. Preheat your air fryer to 350°F (180°C).

2. In a bowl, whisk together the eggs, milk, salt, and pepper.

3. Heat a skillet over medium heat and spray with cooking spray. Add diced bell peppers and onions, and cook until softened.

4. Pour the egg mixture into the skillet with the peppers and onions. Cook, stirring occasionally, until the eggs are scrambled and cooked through.

5. Assemble the burritos by placing a spoonful of scrambled eggs, cooked sausage, and shredded cheese onto each tortilla.

6. Fold the sides of the tortillas over the filling, then roll them up tightly.

7. Lightly spray the air fryer basket with cooking spray. Place the burritos seam side down in the basket, making sure they are not touching.

8. Air fry the burritos for 10-12 minutes, or until golden brown and crispy.

9. Serve hot with your favorite toppings such as salsa, avocado, or sour cream.

MAPLE GLAZED AIR-FRIED DONUTS

- ➢ *Serving Size: 6 donuts*

- ➢ *Cooking Time: 10 minutes*

- ➢ *Prep Time: 15 minutes*

Nutrition Info (per serving):

- *Calories: 180*
- *Fat: 9g*
- *Carbohydrates: 24g*
- *Protein: 2g*

Ingredients:

- *1 can refrigerated biscuit dough*
- *1/4 cup maple syrup*
- *1/4 cup powdered sugar*
- *1 teaspoon vanilla extract*
- *1 tablespoon melted butter*

- Cooking spray

1. **Preheat Air Fryer:** Preheat your air fryer to 350°F (175°C).

2. **Prepare Dough:** Open the can of biscuit dough and separate into individual biscuits. Use a small round cutter to cut out the center of each biscuit to form the donut shape. Save the center holes for donut holes if desired.

3. **Air Fry:** Lightly spray the air fryer basket with cooking spray. Place the donuts in the basket, making sure they don't touch each other. Air fry for 5 minutes, then flip the donuts and air fry for an additional 3-5 minutes until golden brown and cooked through.

4. **Make Glaze:** While the donuts are cooking, mix together the maple syrup, powdered sugar, vanilla extract, and melted butter in a shallow bowl until smooth.

5. **Glaze Donuts:** Once the donuts are done, remove them from the air fryer and immediately dip them into the glaze, coating them evenly. Place the glazed donuts on a wire rack to allow any excess glaze to drip off.

6. **Serve:** Serve the maple glazed air-fried donuts warm and enjoy!

BACON AND EGG STUFFED AVOCADO

> ➢ **Serving Size: 2**

> ➢ **Prep Time: 10 minutes**

> ➢ **Cooking Time: 20 minutes**

Nutrition Info (per serving):

- *Calories: 374*
- *Protein: 13g*
- *Fat: 32g*
- *Carbohydrates: 10g*
- *Fiber: 7g*

Ingredients:

- *2 ripe avocados*
- *4 eggs*
- *4 slices of bacon*
- *Salt and pepper to taste*
- *Optional toppings: chopped chives, shredded cheese, hot sauce*

Directions:

1. Preheat your oven to 425°F (220°C).

2. Cut the avocados in half and remove the pits. If needed, scoop out a bit of flesh to create a larger well for the eggs.

3. Place the avocado halves in a baking dish, using foil to create a stable base if necessary.

4. In a skillet over medium heat, cook the bacon until crispy. Remove from the skillet and drain on paper towels, then crumble into small pieces.

5. Carefully crack an egg into each avocado half, making sure the yolk stays intact. Season with salt and pepper.

6. Place the avocado halves in the oven and bake for about 15-20 minutes, or until the eggs are cooked to your desired doneness.

7. Once the eggs are cooked, remove the avocados from the oven and top with the crumbled bacon and any other desired toppings.

8. Serve immediately and enjoy your delicious bacon and egg stuffed avocados!

CINNAMON SUGAR AIR-FRIED PANCAKE BITES

- ➢ *Serving Size: 4 servings*

- ➢ *Prep Time: 10 minutes*

- ➢ *Cooking Time: 8 minutes*

Nutrition Information (per serving):

- *Calories: 230*
- *Total Fat: 9g*
- *Saturated Fat: 4.5g*
- *Cholesterol: 63mg*
- *Sodium: 360mg*
- *Total Carbohydrates: 33g*
- *Dietary Fiber: 1g*
- *Sugars: 15g*
- *Protein: 5g*

Ingredients:

- *1 cup pancake mix*
- *1/2 cup milk*
- *1 egg*
- *1 teaspoon vanilla extract*
- *2 tablespoons melted butter*
- *1/4 cup granulated sugar*
- *1 teaspoon ground cinnamon*

Directions:

1. In a mixing bowl, combine pancake mix, milk, egg, vanilla extract, and melted butter. Stir until smooth.

2. Preheat your air fryer to 350°F (175°C).
3. Grease the wells of a mini muffin tin.

4. Pour the pancake batter into the wells, filling each about 2/3 full.

5. Place the muffin tin in the air fryer basket and cook for 5-8 minutes, or until the pancake bites are golden brown and cooked through.

6. While the pancake bites are cooking, mix together the granulated sugar and ground cinnamon in a small bowl.

7. Once the pancake bites are cooked, immediately remove them from the air fryer and roll them in the cinnamon sugar mixture until evenly coated.

8. Serve warm and enjoy!

VEGGIE AND CHEESE MINI FRITTATAS

- ➢ *Serving Size: Makes 12 mini frittatas*

- ➢ *Prep Time: 15 minutes*

- ➢ *Cooking Time: 20 minutes*

Nutrition Info (per mini frittata):
- Calories: 90
- Fat: 6g
- Carbohydrates: 2g

- Protein: 7g

Ingredients:

- 6 large eggs
- 1/4 cup milk
- 1/2 cup shredded cheese (cheddar, mozzarella, or your choice)
- 1/4 cup diced bell peppers
- 1/4 cup diced onions
- 1/4 cup diced tomatoes
- Salt and pepper to taste
- Cooking spray or olive oil for greasing

Directions:

1. Preheat your oven to 375°F (190°C). Grease a 12-cup muffin tin with cooking spray or olive oil.

2. In a mixing bowl, whisk together eggs, milk, salt, and pepper until well combined.

3. Stir in shredded cheese, diced bell peppers, onions, and tomatoes.

4. Pour the egg mixture evenly into the prepared muffin tin, filling each cup about 3/4 full.

5. Bake in the preheated oven for 15-20 minutes, or until the frittatas are set and the edges are golden brown.

6. Remove from the oven and let cool for a few minutes before carefully removing the frittatas from the muffin tin.

7. Serve warm or at room temperature, and enjoy your delicious veggie and cheese mini frittatas!

CHAPTER 2

APPETIZERS AND SNACKS

CRISPY AIR FRYER BUFFALO CAULIFLOWER BITES

> ➢ *Serving Size: This recipe serves 4.*

> ➢ *Cooking Time: Approximately 20 minutes.*

> ➢ *Prep Time: About 10 minutes.*

Nutrition Info: (Per serving)

- Calories: 120
- Total Fat: 5g
- Saturated Fat: 1g
- Cholesterol: 0mg
- Sodium: 720mg
- Total Carbohydrates: 18g
- Dietary Fiber: 6g
- Sugars: 5g
- Protein: 5g

Ingredients:

- 1 head of cauliflower, cut into bite-sized florets

- 1/2 cup all-purpose flour
- 1/2 cup water
- 1 teaspoon garlic powder
- 1/2 teaspoon salt
- 1/4 teaspoon black pepper
- 1/2 cup buffalo sauce
- 2 tablespoons melted butter or olive oil

Directions:

1. Preheat your air fryer to 375°F (190°C).

2. In a mixing bowl, combine the all-purpose flour, water, garlic powder, salt, and black pepper to create a batter.

3. Dip each cauliflower floret into the batter, ensuring it's well-coated, and shake off any excess batter.

4. Place the coated cauliflower florets in the air fryer basket, making sure they are not overcrowded.

5. Cook in the air fryer for about 15 minutes, flipping halfway through, or until the cauliflower is golden brown and crispy.

6. In a separate bowl, mix the buffalo sauce with melted butter or olive oil.

7. Once the cauliflower is done, transfer it to a large mixing bowl and pour the buffalo sauce mixture over it. Gently toss until the cauliflower is evenly coated.

8. Return the coated cauliflower to the air fryer basket and cook for an additional 5 minutes to allow the sauce to caramelize slightly.

9. Once done, remove the buffalo cauliflower bites from the air fryer and serve hot with your favorite dipping sauce or enjoy them as is.

GARLIC PARMESAN AIR FRYER ZUCCHINI CHIPS

> *Serving Size: 4 servings*

> *Cooking Time: 10-12 minutes*

> *Prep Time: 15 minutes*

Nutrition Info (per serving):

- Calories: 120
- Total Fat: 8g
- Saturated Fat: 2g
- Cholesterol: 5mg
- Sodium: 220mg
- Total Carbohydrates: 9g
- Dietary Fiber: 2g
- Sugars: 2g
- Protein: 5g
Ingredients:

- 2 medium zucchinis, thinly sliced
- 1/2 cup grated Parmesan cheese
- 1/4 cup bread crumbs
- 1 teaspoon garlic powder
- 1/2 teaspoon onion powder
- 1/2 teaspoon paprika
- Salt and pepper to taste
- Cooking spray

Directions:

1. Preheat your air fryer to 375°F (190°C).

2. In a shallow dish, combine Parmesan cheese, bread crumbs, garlic powder, onion powder, paprika, salt, and pepper.

3. Dip each zucchini slice into the Parmesan mixture, coating both sides evenly.

4. Lightly spray the air fryer basket with cooking spray.

5. Place the coated zucchini slices in a single layer in the air fryer basket, making sure they're not overlapping.

6. Cook in the air fryer for 5-6 minutes, then flip the zucchini slices and cook for an additional 5-6 minutes, or until golden brown and crispy.

7. Remove from the air fryer and let cool slightly before serving.

8. Enjoy your crispy Garlic Parmesan Air Fryer Zucchini Chips as a tasty snack or side dish!

SPICY SRIRACHA AIR FRYER CHICKEN WINGS

- ➢ *Serving Size: 4 servings*

- ➢ *Prep Time: 10 minutes*

- ➢ *Cooking Time: 20 minutes*

Nutrition Info (per serving):

- *Calories: 280*
- *Fat: 18g*
- *Carbohydrates: 5g*
- *Protein: 24g*

Ingredients:

- *1 lb chicken wings, split at joints, tips removed*
- *2 tablespoons Sriracha sauce*
- *1 tablespoon soy sauce*
- *1 tablespoon olive oil*
- *1 teaspoon garlic powder*
- *1 teaspoon onion powder*
- *1/2 teaspoon paprika*

- Salt and pepper to taste
- Optional: sesame seeds and chopped green onions for garnish

Directions:

1. Preheat your air fryer to 380°F (190°C).

2. In a bowl, mix together Sriracha sauce, soy sauce, olive oil, garlic powder, onion powder, paprika, salt, and pepper.

3. Pat the chicken wings dry with paper towels and place them in a large mixing bowl.

4. Pour the Sriracha sauce mixture over the chicken wings and toss until evenly coated.

5. Place the chicken wings in the air fryer basket in a single layer, making sure they are not touching each other.

6. Air fry the chicken wings for 10 minutes, then flip them over and air fry for another 10 minutes, or until they are cooked through and crispy.

7. Once cooked, transfer the chicken wings to a serving plate and garnish with sesame seeds and chopped green onions if desired.

8. Serve hot and enjoy your spicy Sriracha air fryer chicken wings!

MOZZARELLA STICKS WITH MARINARA SAUCE

- ➤ *Serving Size: 4 servings*

- ➤ *Prep Time: 15 minutes*

- ➤ *Cooking Time: 10 minutes*

Nutrition Info (per serving):

- Calories: 280
- Total Fat: 15g
- Saturated Fat: 7g
- Cholesterol: 30mg
- Sodium: 710mg
- Total Carbohydrates: 22g
- Dietary Fiber: 2g
- Sugars: 4g
- Protein: 13g

Ingredients:

- 12 sticks of string cheese
- 1 cup Italian breadcrumbs
- ½ cup all-purpose flour
- 2 large eggs, beaten
- 1 cup marinara sauce
- Cooking spray

Directions:

1. Prepare the Cheese Sticks: Cut each string cheese stick in half to make 24 pieces.

2. Breading Station: Set up a breading station with three shallow dishes. Place the flour in one dish, beaten eggs in another, and breadcrumbs in the third dish.

3. Coat the Cheese: Dip each cheese stick into the flour, shaking off any excess. Then dip it into the beaten egg, allowing any excess to drip off. Finally, coat it evenly with breadcrumbs, pressing gently to adhere.

4. Freeze: Place the breaded cheese sticks on a baking sheet lined with parchment paper.
Freeze them for at least 30 minutes. This step helps the breading adhere during frying.

5. Fry the Mozzarella Sticks: In a deep skillet, heat oil over medium-high heat. Carefully add the frozen cheese sticks in batches, frying until golden brown, about 1-2 minutes per side. Transfer them to a paper towel-lined plate to drain excess oil.

6. Serve: Serve the mozzarella sticks hot with marinara sauce for dipping.

CRISPY AIR FRYER ONION RINGS

  ➢ *Serving Size: 4 servings*

➢ **Cooking Time: 12-15 minutes**

➢ **Prep Time:15 minutes**

Nutrition Info: (Per serving)

- *Calories: 150*
- *Total Fat: 6g*
- *Saturated Fat: 1g*
- *Cholesterol: 0mg*
- *Sodium: 250mg*
- *Total Carbohydrates: 23g*
- *Dietary Fiber: 2g*
- *Sugars: 5g*
- *Protein: 3g*

Ingredients:

- *2 large onions, cut into 1/2-inch rings*
- *1 cup all-purpose flour*
- *1 teaspoon garlic powder*
- *1 teaspoon paprika*
- *1/2 teaspoon salt*
- *1/4 teaspoon black pepper*
- *2 eggs, beaten*
- *1 cup breadcrumbs*
- *Cooking spray*

Directions:

1. Preheat Air Fryer: Preheat your air fryer to 370°F (190°C).

2. Prepare Onions: Separate the onion slices into rings and set aside.

3. Prepare Coating: In a shallow dish, mix together the flour, garlic powder, paprika, salt, and black pepper. In another dish, place the beaten eggs. In a third dish, add the breadcrumbs.

4. Coat Onion Rings: Dip each onion ring into the flour mixture, shaking off any excess. Then dip it into the beaten eggs, followed by the breadcrumbs, ensuring each ring is evenly coated.

5. Air Fry: Lightly coat the air fryer basket with cooking spray. Arrange the coated onion rings in a single layer in the basket, making sure they do not overlap. Spray the tops of the onion rings with cooking spray.

6. Cook: Air fry the onion rings in batches for 6-8 minutes, or until golden brown and crispy, flipping halfway through the cooking time.

7. Serve: Once cooked, transfer the crispy onion rings to a serving plate and serve immediately with your favorite dipping sauce.

BBQ BACON WRAPPED JALAPEÑO POPPERS

 ➢ *Serving Size: 12 poppers*

➢ **Prep Time: 15 minutes**

➢ **Cooking Time: 20 minutes**

Nutrition Info (per serving):

- *Calories: 150*
- *Total Fat: 11g*
- *Cholesterol: 25mg*
- *Sodium: 290mg*
- *Total Carbohydrates: 5g*
- *Protein: 7g*

Ingredients:

- *6 large jalapeño peppers, halved and seeded*
- *6 slices of bacon, cut in half*
- *6 ounces cream cheese, softened*
- *1/4 cup shredded cheddar cheese*
- *1/4 cup BBQ sauce*
- *Toothpicks*

Directions:

1. Preheat your grill to medium-high heat or set your oven to 400°F (200°C).

2. In a small bowl, mix the cream cheese and shredded cheddar cheese until well combined.

3. Fill each jalapeño half with the cheese mixture, then wrap each filled jalapeño half with a half slice of bacon. Secure the bacon with a toothpick.

4. Place the bacon-wrapped jalapeño poppers on the grill or a baking sheet if using the oven.

5. Grill or bake the poppers for about 15-20 minutes, or until the bacon is crispy and the jalapeños are tender.

6. During the last 5 minutes of cooking, brush the poppers with BBQ sauce, allowing it to caramelize.

7. Once cooked, remove the poppers from the grill or oven and let them cool for a few minutes before serving.

8. Enjoy your delicious BBQ Bacon Wrapped Jalapeño Poppers as a savory appetizer or snack!

CHAPTER 3

MAIN COURSES

CRISPY AIR-FRIED CHICKEN TENDERS

- ➢ *Serving Size: 4 servings*

- ➢ *Prep Time: 15 minutes*

- ➢ *Cooking Time: 12 minutes*

Nutrition Info (per serving):

- Calories: 220
- Total Fat: 8g
- Saturated Fat: 2g
- Cholesterol: 80mg
- Sodium: 560mg
- Total Carbohydrates: 8g
- Dietary Fiber: 1g
- Sugars: 1g
- Protein: 29g

Ingredients:

- 1 lb chicken tenders
- 1 cup all-purpose flour

- *2 large eggs, beaten*
- *1 cup breadcrumbs*
- *1/2 cup grated Parmesan cheese*
- *1 tsp garlic powder*
- *1 tsp paprika*
- *1/2 tsp salt*
- *1/2 tsp black pepper*
- *Cooking spray*

Directions:

1. Preheat your air fryer to 400°F (200°C).

2. In three separate bowls, place the flour in one, beaten eggs in another, and mix breadcrumbs, Parmesan cheese, garlic powder, paprika, salt, and black pepper in the third.

3. Dredge each chicken tender in the flour, then dip into the beaten eggs, and finally coat with the breadcrumb mixture, pressing gently to adhere.

4. Lightly spray the air fryer basket with cooking spray to prevent sticking.

5. Place the coated chicken tenders in a single layer in the air fryer basket, making sure they are not touching each other.

6. Cook in the preheated air fryer for 10-12 minutes, flipping halfway through cooking, until the chicken is golden brown and cooked through with an internal temperature of 165°F (75°C).

7. Once cooked, transfer the chicken tenders to a plate and serve hot with your favorite dipping sauce.

FLAVORFUL AIR-FRIED SALMON FILLETS

➢ *Serving Size: 2 servings*

➢ *Prep Time: 10 minutes*

➢ *Cooking Time: 10 minutes*

Nutrition Info (per serving):

- Calories: 250
- Protein: 25g
- Fat: 15g
- Carbohydrates: 0g
- Fiber: 0g
- Sodium: 400mg

Ingredients:

- 2 salmon fillets (about 6 ounces each), skin-on or skinless
- 1 tablespoon olive oil
- 1 teaspoon garlic powder

- 1 teaspoon paprika
- 1/2 teaspoon salt
- 1/4 teaspoon black pepper
- Lemon wedges, for serving
- Fresh herbs (optional), for garnish

Directions:

1. Preheat your air fryer to 400°F (200°C) for 5 minutes.

2. In a small bowl, mix together the olive oil, garlic powder, paprika, salt, and black pepper to create a seasoning mixture.

3. Pat the salmon fillets dry with paper towels. Rub the seasoning mixture evenly over both sides of the salmon fillets.

4. Place the seasoned salmon fillets in the air fryer basket, skin-side down if using skin-on fillets.

5. Air fry the salmon fillets at 400°F (200°C) for 8-10 minutes, depending on the thickness of the fillets. The salmon is done when it easily flakes with a fork and reaches an internal temperature of 145°F (63°C).

6. Carefully remove the salmon fillets from the air fryer and transfer them to serving plates.

7. Serve the air-fried salmon fillets hot with lemon wedges on the side for squeezing over the fish. Garnish with fresh herbs if desired.

8. Enjoy your flavorful and perfectly cooked air-fried salmon fillets!

JUICY AIR-FRIED TURKEY BURGERS

> *Serving Size: 4 burgers*

> *Prep Time: 10 minutes*

> *Cooking Time: 15 minutes*

> *Total Time: 25 minutes*

Nutrition Info (per serving):

- Calories: 250
- Protein: 30g
- Fat: 12g
- Carbohydrates: 6g
- Fiber: 1g
- Sugars: 1g

Ingredients:

- 1 pound ground turkey
- 1/4 cup breadcrumbs
- 1/4 cup finely chopped onion
- 2 cloves garlic, minced
- 1 tablespoon Worcestershire sauce
- 1 teaspoon Dijon mustard
- 1/2 teaspoon salt
- 1/4 teaspoon black pepper
- 4 whole wheat burger buns
- Optional toppings: lettuce, tomato, avocado, cheese

Directions:

1. Preheat your air fryer to 375°F (190°C).

2. In a large bowl, combine the ground turkey, breadcrumbs, onion, garlic, Worcestershire sauce, mustard, salt, and pepper. Mix until well combined.

3. Divide the mixture into 4 equal portions and shape each portion into a patty.

4. Place the turkey patties in the preheated air fryer basket, leaving some space between each patty.

5. Cook the patties in the air fryer for 12-15 minutes, flipping halfway through, until they are cooked through and reach an internal temperature of 165°F (75°C).

6. While the patties are cooking, lightly toast the burger buns if desired.

7. Once the turkey burgers are cooked, assemble your burgers by placing each patty on a bun and adding your favorite toppings.

8. Serve the juicy air-fried turkey burgers immediately and enjoy!

DELICIOUS AIR-FRIED SHRIMP SCAMPI

- ➢ *Serving Size: 4 servings*

- ➢ *Prep Time: 10 minutes*

- ➢ *Cooking Time: 10 minutes*

Nutrition Info (per serving):

- Calories: 220
- Fat: 10g
- Carbohydrates: 8g
- Protein: 25g

Ingredients:

- 1 pound large shrimp, peeled and deveined
- 2 tablespoons olive oil
- 4 cloves garlic, minced
- 1/4 cup chopped fresh parsley
- 1/4 teaspoon red pepper flakes (optional)
- Salt and black pepper to taste
- 2 tablespoons freshly squeezed lemon juice
- 2 tablespoons grated Parmesan cheese

Directions:

1. Preheat your air fryer to 400°F (200°C).

2. In a large bowl, toss the shrimp with olive oil, minced garlic, chopped parsley, red pepper flakes (if using), salt, and black pepper until well coated.

3. Place the seasoned shrimp in the air fryer basket in a single layer. You may need to cook them in batches depending on the size of your air fryer.

4. Air fry the shrimp for 6-8 minutes, shaking the basket halfway through cooking, until they are pink and cooked through.

5. Once the shrimp are cooked, transfer them to a serving dish and drizzle with freshly squeezed lemon juice.

6. Sprinkle grated Parmesan cheese over the shrimp and serve immediately.

TENDER AIR-FRIED PORK CHOPS

- ➢ *Serving Size: 4 servings*

- ➢ *Cooking Time: 20 minutes*

- ➢ *Prep Time: 10 minutes*

Nutrition Info (per serving):

- *Calories: 250*
- *Total Fat: 12g*
- *Saturated Fat: 3.5g*
- *Cholesterol: 90mg*
- *Sodium: 400mg*
- *Total Carbohydrates: 2g*
- *Dietary Fiber: 0g*
- *Sugars: 0g*
- *Protein: 30g*

Ingredients:

- *4 boneless pork chops, about 1 inch thick*
- *2 tablespoons olive oil*
- *1 teaspoon garlic powder*
- *1 teaspoon onion powder*
- *1 teaspoon paprika*
- *1 teaspoon dried thyme*
- *Salt and pepper to taste*

Directions:

1. Preheat the Air Fryer: Preheat your air fryer to 400°F (200°C) for about 3-5 minutes.

2. Prepare the Pork Chops: Pat the pork chops dry with paper towels to remove excess moisture. In a small bowl, mix together the olive oil, garlic powder, onion powder, paprika, dried thyme, salt, and pepper.

3. Season the Pork Chops: Brush both sides of the pork chops with the olive oil mixture, ensuring they are evenly coated.

4. Air Fry the Pork Chops: Place the pork chops in the air fryer basket in a single layer, making sure they are not overcrowded. Cook for 10 minutes, then flip the pork chops over and cook for an additional 5-7 minutes, or until they reach an internal temperature of 145°F (63°C) for medium doneness.

5. Rest and Serve: Once cooked, remove the pork chops from the air fryer and let them rest for a few minutes before serving. This allows the juices to redistribute, ensuring juicy and tender pork chops.

6. Enjoy: Serve the air-fried pork chops hot with your favorite side dishes, such as roasted vegetables, mashed potatoes, or a crisp salad.

SPICY AIR-FRIED VEGGIE STIR-FRY

> ➢ *Serving Size: 2 servings*

> ➢ *Prep Time: 10 minutes*

> ➢ *Cooking Time: 15 minutes*

Nutrition Info (per serving):

- *Calories: 150*
- *Total Fat: 8g*
- *Saturated Fat: 1g*
- *Cholesterol: 0mg*
- *Sodium: 300mg*
- *Total Carbohydrates: 18g*
- *Dietary Fiber: 7g*
- *Sugars: 8g*
- *Protein: 5g*

Ingredients:

- *2 cups mixed vegetables (such as bell peppers, broccoli, carrots, snap peas)*
- *1 tablespoon olive oil*
- *2 cloves garlic, minced*
- *1 teaspoon grated ginger*
- *2 tablespoons soy sauce*
- *1 tablespoon sriracha sauce (adjust to taste)*
- *1 tablespoon honey or maple syrup*

- 1 teaspoon sesame oil
- Salt and pepper to taste
- Sesame seeds and chopped green onions for garnish (optional)

Directions:

1. Preheat your air fryer to 380°F (190°C).

2. In a small bowl, whisk together the garlic, ginger, soy sauce, sriracha sauce, honey (or maple syrup), and sesame oil to make the sauce. Set aside.

3. Place the mixed vegetables in a large mixing bowl. Drizzle with olive oil and toss to coat evenly.

4. Transfer the seasoned vegetables to the air fryer basket, spreading them out in a single layer.

5. Air fry the vegetables for 8-10 minutes, shaking the basket halfway through cooking, until they are tender and slightly charred.

6. Once the vegetables are cooked, transfer them back to the mixing bowl. Pour the prepared sauce over the hot vegetables and toss until evenly coated.

7. Serve the spicy air-fried veggie stir-fry immediately, garnished with sesame seeds and chopped green onions if desired.

CHAPTER 4

SIDES AND ACCOMPANIMENTS

CRISPY AIR-FRIED CHICKEN WINGS

- ➤ *Serving Size: 4 servings*

- ➤ *Prep Time: 10 minutes*

- ➤ *Cooking Time: 20 minutes*

Nutrition Info (per serving):

- *Calories: 250*
- *Protein: 25g*
- *Carbohydrates: 0g*
- *Fat: 16g*
- *Fiber: 0g*
- *Sugar: 0g*
- *Sodium: 450mg*

Ingredients:

- *2 lbs chicken wings*
- *1 tablespoon baking powder*
- *1 teaspoon salt*

- 1 teaspoon black pepper
- Optional: your favorite seasoning blend (such as garlic powder, paprika, or cayenne pepper)

Directions:

1. Preheat your air fryer to 400°F (200°C).

2. Pat the chicken wings dry with paper towels to remove excess moisture.

3. In a large bowl, mix together the baking powder, salt, pepper, and any optional seasonings.

4. Add the chicken wings to the bowl and toss them in the seasoning mixture until evenly coated.

5. Place the chicken wings in the air fryer basket in a single layer, making sure they are not touching each other.

6. Cook the wings in the air fryer for 10 minutes.

7. After 10 minutes, flip the wings over using tongs and cook for an additional 10 minutes, or until they are golden brown and crispy.

8. Once cooked, remove the wings from the air fryer and let them rest for a few minutes before serving.

9. Serve the crispy air-fried chicken wings hot with your favorite dipping sauce or enjoy them as is.

FLAVORFUL SWEET POTATO FRIES

➢ *Serving Size: 4 servings*

➢ *Prep Time: 10 minutes*

➢ *Cooking Time: 20 minutes*

Nutrition Info (per serving):

- *Calories: 150*
- *Total Fat: 7g*
- *Saturated Fat: 1g*
- *Cholesterol: 0mg*
- *Sodium: 200mg*
- *Total Carbohydrates: 22g*
- *Dietary Fiber: 3g*
- *Sugars: 6g*
- *Protein: 2g*

Ingredients:

- *2 large sweet potatoes, peeled and cut into fries*
- *2 tablespoons olive oil*
- *1 teaspoon garlic powder*
- *1 teaspoon paprika*
- *1/2 teaspoon salt*
- *1/4 teaspoon black pepper*
- *Optional: 1/4 teaspoon cayenne pepper for a spicy kick*

<u>*Directions:*</u>

1. Preheat your oven to 425°F (220°C) and line a baking sheet with parchment paper.

2. In a large bowl, toss the sweet potato fries with olive oil until evenly coated.

3. In a small bowl, mix together the garlic powder, paprika, salt, black pepper, and cayenne pepper (if using).

4. Sprinkle the spice mixture over the sweet potato fries and toss until they are evenly seasoned.

5. Spread the seasoned sweet potato fries out in a single layer on the prepared baking sheet.

6. Bake in the preheated oven for 15-20 minutes, flipping halfway through, until the fries are golden brown and crispy.

7. Serve hot and enjoy your flavorful sweet potato fries!

ZESTY GARLIC PARMESAN BRUSSELS SPROUTS

- ➢ *Serving Size: 4 servings*

- ➢ *Prep Time: 10 minutes*

> ➤ **Cooking Time: 20 minutes**

Nutrition Info (per serving):

- *Calories: 150*
- *Fat: 8g*
- *Carbohydrates: 12g*
- *Protein: 8g*
- *Fiber: 4g*

Ingredients:

- *1 lb Brussels sprouts, trimmed and halved*
- *2 tablespoons olive oil*
- *3 cloves garlic, minced*
- *1/4 cup grated Parmesan cheese*
- *1 teaspoon lemon zest*
- *Salt and pepper to taste*

Directions:

1. Preheat your oven to 400°F (200°C).

2. In a large bowl, toss the Brussels sprouts with olive oil, minced garlic, salt, and pepper until evenly coated.

3. Spread the Brussels sprouts out on a baking sheet in a single layer.

4. Roast in the preheated oven for 15-20 minutes, or until the Brussels sprouts are tender and browned, stirring halfway through.

5. Once cooked, remove the Brussels sprouts from the oven and transfer them back to the bowl.

6. Sprinkle the grated Parmesan cheese and lemon zest over the roasted Brussels sprouts and toss to coat evenly.

7. Serve immediately as a delicious side dish or appetizer.

SPICY BUFFALO CAULIFLOWER BITES

➢ *Serving Size: 4 servings*

➢ *Prep Time: 15 minutes*

➢ *Cooking Time: 25 minutes*

Nutrition Info (per serving):

- *Calories: 150*
- *Total Fat: 6g*
- *Saturated Fat: 1g*
- *Cholesterol: 0mg*

- Sodium: 720mg
- Total Carbohydrates: 21g
- Dietary Fiber: 6g
- Sugars: 3g
- Protein: 6g

Ingredients:

- 1 head of cauliflower, cut into florets
- 1/2 cup all-purpose flour
- 1/2 cup water
- 1 teaspoon garlic powder
- 1/2 teaspoon salt
- 1/4 teaspoon black pepper
- 1/2 cup buffalo sauce
- 2 tablespoons melted butter or olive oil
- Optional: ranch or blue cheese dressing for dipping

Directions:

1. Preheat your oven to 450°F (230°C) and line a baking sheet with parchment paper or lightly grease it.

2. In a large bowl, mix together the flour, water, garlic powder, salt, and black pepper until smooth.

3. Toss the cauliflower florets in the batter until evenly coated.

4. Place the coated cauliflower on the prepared baking sheet in a single layer, making sure they are not touching each other.

5. Bake for 20-25 minutes, or until the cauliflower is golden brown and crispy.

6. In a separate bowl, mix together the buffalo sauce and melted butter or olive oil.

7. Once the cauliflower is done, remove it from the oven and carefully toss it in the buffalo sauce mixture until evenly coated.

8. Return the cauliflower to the baking sheet and bake for an additional 5 minutes.

9. Remove from the oven and let cool for a few minutes before serving.

10. Serve hot with ranch or blue cheese dressing for dipping, if desired.

CHAPTER 5

VEGETARIAN AND VEGAN OPTIONS

CRISPY AIR-FRIED TOFU NUGGETS

- ➢ *Serving Size: 4 servings*

- ➢ *Prep Time: 15 minutes*

- ➢ *Cooking Time: 15 minutes*

Nutrition Info (per serving):

- *Calories: 150*
- *Total Fat: 8g*
- *Saturated Fat: 1g*
- *Cholesterol: 0mg*
- *Sodium: 300mg*
- *Total Carbohydrates: 10g*
- *Dietary Fiber: 3g*
- *Sugars: 1g*
- *Protein: 12g*

Ingredients:

- *1 block of firm tofu (about 14 ounces), pressed and drained*

- 2 tablespoons soy sauce
- 1 tablespoon rice vinegar
- 1 teaspoon garlic powder
- 1 teaspoon onion powder
- 1/2 teaspoon paprika
- 1/4 teaspoon black pepper
- 1/2 cup cornstarch
- Cooking spray

Directions:

1. Preheat your air fryer to 400°F (200°C).

2. Cut the pressed tofu into bite-sized nuggets or cubes.

3. In a shallow bowl, whisk together the soy sauce, rice vinegar, garlic powder, onion powder, paprika, and black pepper.

4. Dip each tofu nugget into the marinade, making sure to coat all sides evenly.

5. Place the cornstarch in another shallow bowl. Dredge each marinated tofu nugget in the cornstarch until well coated.

6. Lightly spray the air fryer basket with cooking spray to prevent sticking.

7. Arrange the coated tofu nuggets in a single layer in the air fryer basket, making sure they are not touching each other.

8. Air fry for 12-15 minutes, flipping halfway through, until the tofu is golden brown and crispy.

9. Serve hot with your favorite dipping sauce and enjoy your crispy air-fried tofu nuggets!

ZUCCHINI FRIES WITH VEGAN DIPPING SAUCE

> *Serving Size: 4 servings*

> *Prep Time: 15 minutes*

> *Cooking Time: 20 minutes*

Nutrition Info (per serving):

- Calories: 180
- Total Fat: 9g
- Saturated Fat: 1g
- Cholesterol: 0mg
- Sodium: 380mg
- Total Carbohydrates: 22g
- Dietary Fiber: 3g
- Sugars: 4g

- Protein: 5g

- 2 medium zucchinis
- 1 cup breadcrumbs
- 2 tablespoons nutritional yeast
- 1 teaspoon garlic powder
- 1 teaspoon onion powder
- 1/2 teaspoon paprika
- Salt and pepper to taste
- Vegan dipping sauce of your choice

Directions:

1. Preheat your oven to 425°F (220°C). Line a baking sheet with parchment paper.

2. Wash and dry the zucchinis. Cut off the ends and slice them lengthwise into fries-like shapes, about 1/2 inch thick.

3. In a shallow dish, mix together breadcrumbs, nutritional yeast, garlic powder, onion powder, paprika, salt, and pepper.

4. Dip each zucchini fry into the breadcrumb mixture, coating evenly on all sides, and place them on the prepared baking sheet.

5. Once all the fries are coated and arranged on the baking sheet, lightly spray them with cooking spray or drizzle with olive oil.

6. Bake in the preheated oven for 15-20 minutes, flipping halfway through, until the fries are golden brown and crispy.

7. While the fries are baking, prepare your favorite vegan dipping sauce.

8. Once the zucchini fries are done, remove them from the oven and let them cool for a few minutes before serving with the dipping sauce.

PORTOBELLO MUSHROOM BURGERS WITH AVOCADO SLICES

- ➤ *Serving Size: 2 burgers*

- ➤ *Prep Time: 10 minutes*

- ➤ *Cooking Time: 15 minutes*

Nutrition Info (per serving):

- Calories: 320
- Protein: 8g

- *Fat: 25g*
- *Carbohydrates: 20g*
- *Fiber: 10g*

Ingredients:

- *2 large Portobello mushrooms, stems removed*
- *1 ripe avocado, sliced*
- *2 whole grain burger buns*
- *2 tablespoons olive oil*
- *2 cloves garlic, minced*
- *1 teaspoon dried thyme*
- *Salt and pepper to taste*
- *Optional toppings: lettuce, tomato, onion, cheese*

Directions:

1. Preheat your grill or grill pan over medium heat.

2. In a small bowl, mix together olive oil, minced garlic, dried thyme, salt, and pepper.

3. Brush both sides of the Portobello mushrooms with the olive oil mixture.

4. Place the mushrooms on the grill and cook for about 5-7 minutes on each side, or until tender.

5. While the mushrooms are grilling, toast the burger buns on the grill for a minute or two until lightly golden.

6. Assemble your burgers by placing a grilled Portobello mushroom on the bottom half of each bun.

7. Top each mushroom with avocado slices and any other desired toppings.

8. Place the top half of the bun on top and serve immediately.

BUFFALO CAULIFLOWER WINGS

> ➢ *Serving Size: 4 servings*

> ➢ *Cooking Time: 25 minutes*

> ➢ *Prep Time: 15 minutes*

Nutrition Info (per serving):

- *Calories: 150*
- *Total Fat: 8g*
- *Saturated Fat: 1g*
- *Cholesterol: 0mg*
- *Sodium: 700mg*
- *Total Carbohydrates: 17g*
- *Dietary Fiber: 5g*
- *Sugars: 3g*
- *Protein: 5g*

Ingredients:

- 1 head of cauliflower, cut into florets
- 1 cup of all-purpose flour
- 1 cup of water
- 1 teaspoon of garlic powder
- 1 teaspoon of onion powder
- 1/2 teaspoon of paprika
- Salt and pepper to taste
- 1 cup of buffalo sauce
- 2 tablespoons of melted butter or olive oil

Directions:

1. Preheat your oven to 450°F (230°C). Line a baking sheet with parchment paper or lightly grease it.

2. In a mixing bowl, combine the flour, water, garlic powder, onion powder, paprika, salt, and pepper. Stir until smooth and well combined.

3. Dip each cauliflower floret into the batter, coating it completely, then place it on the prepared baking sheet. Repeat until all florets are coated.

4. Bake the cauliflower in the preheated oven for 15-20 minutes, or until golden brown and crispy.

5. In a separate bowl, mix together the buffalo sauce and melted butter or olive oil.

6. Once the cauliflower is done baking, remove it from the oven and transfer it to a large mixing bowl.

7. Pour the buffalo sauce mixture over the cauliflower and toss until evenly coated.

8. Return the cauliflower to the baking sheet and bake for an additional 5 minutes, or until the sauce is slightly caramelized.

9. Serve hot with your favorite dipping sauce and enjoy your delicious Buffalo Cauliflower Wings!

STUFFED BELL PEPPERS WITH QUINOA AND BLACK BEANS

- ➤ *Serving Size: 4 servings*

- ➤ *Prep Time: 15 minutes*

- ➤ *Cooking Time: 40 minutes*

Nutrition Info (per serving):

- Calories: 320
- Total Fat: 5g
- Saturated Fat: 1g
- Cholesterol: 0mg
- Sodium: 480mg

- Total Carbohydrates: 58g
- Dietary Fiber: 12g
- Sugars: 8g
- Protein: 14g

Ingredients:

- 4 large bell peppers (any color)
- 1 cup quinoa, rinsed
- 1 can (15 ounces) black beans, drained and rinsed
- 1 cup corn kernels (fresh, frozen, or canned)
- 1 cup diced tomatoes
- 1 small onion, finely chopped
- 2 cloves garlic, minced
- 1 teaspoon ground cumin
- 1 teaspoon chili powder
- Salt and pepper to taste
- 1 cup shredded cheese (optional, for topping)
- Fresh cilantro for garnish (optional)

Directions:

1. Preheat your oven to 375°F (190°C).

2. Cut the tops off the bell peppers and remove the seeds and membranes. Rinse them under cold water and set aside.

3. In a medium saucepan, bring 2 cups of water to a boil. Add the quinoa, reduce heat to low, cover, and simmer for

about 15 minutes, or until the quinoa is cooked and water is absorbed. Remove from heat and fluff with a fork.

4. In a large skillet, heat some olive oil over medium heat. Add the chopped onion and garlic, and sauté until softened, about 3-4 minutes.

5. Stir in the cooked quinoa, black beans, corn, diced tomatoes, ground cumin, chili powder, salt, and pepper. Cook for another 5 minutes, allowing the flavors to meld together. Taste and adjust seasonings if needed.

6. Place the bell peppers upright in a baking dish. Fill each pepper with the quinoa and black bean mixture, pressing down gently to pack it in.

7. If using cheese, sprinkle it over the stuffed peppers.

8. Cover the baking dish with aluminum foil and bake in the preheated oven for 25-30 minutes, or until the peppers are tender.

9. Once cooked, remove the foil and bake for an additional 5 minutes to melt the cheese and lightly brown the tops.

10. Garnish with fresh cilantro if desired, and serve hot.

AIR-FRIED VEGETABLE SPRING ROLLS WITH SWEET CHILI DIPPING SAUCE

- ➢ *Serving Size: 4 servings*

- ➢ *Cooking Time: 15 minutes*

- ➢ *Prep Time: 20 minutes*

Nutrition Info:

- *Calories: 150 per serving*
- *Total Fat: 4g*
- *Saturated Fat: 1g*
- *Cholesterol: 0mg*
- *Sodium: 350mg*
- *Total Carbohydrates: 25g*
- *Dietary Fiber: 3g*
- *Sugars: 6g*
- *Protein: 5g*

Ingredients:

- *8 spring roll wrappers*
- *2 cups shredded cabbage*
- *1 cup shredded carrots*
- *1 cup thinly sliced bell peppers*
- *1 cup bean sprouts*
- *2 tablespoons soy sauce*
- *1 tablespoon sesame oil*

- 1 tablespoon cornstarch mixed with 2 tablespoons water (for sealing rolls)
- Cooking spray

- 1/4 cup sweet chili sauce
- 1 tablespoon soy sauce
- 1 tablespoon rice vinegar
- 1 teaspoon minced garlic
- 1 teaspoon minced ginger

Directions:

1. In a large bowl, combine shredded cabbage, carrots, bell peppers, bean sprouts, soy sauce, and sesame oil. Mix well.

2. Lay a spring roll wrapper on a clean surface. Place about 1/4 cup of the vegetable mixture in the center of the wrapper.

3. Fold the bottom edge of the wrapper over the filling, then fold in the sides, and roll tightly.

4. Use the cornstarch mixture to seal the edge of the wrapper.

5. Repeat with the remaining wrappers and filling.

6. Preheat the air fryer to 375°F (190°C).

7. Lightly coat the spring rolls with cooking spray.

8. Place the spring rolls in the air fryer basket in a single layer, making sure they are not touching.

9. Air fry for 10-12 minutes, flipping halfway through, until golden brown and crispy.

10. While the spring rolls are cooking, prepare the dipping sauce by combining sweet chili sauce, soy sauce, rice vinegar, minced garlic, and minced ginger in a small bowl.

11. Serve the air-fried vegetable spring rolls hot with the sweet chili dipping sauce on the side.

CHAPTER 6

SWEET TREATS

CINNAMON SUGAR DONUT HOLES

- ➢ *Serving Size: Approximately 24 donut holes*

- ➢ *Prep Time: 15 minutes*

- ➢ *Cooking Time: 10 minutes*

Nutrition Information (per serving):

- *Calories: 90*
- *Total Fat: 3g*
- *Saturated Fat: 2g*
- *Cholesterol: 15mg*
- *Sodium: 100mg*
- *Total Carbohydrates: 14g*
- *Dietary Fiber: 0.5g*
- *Sugars: 7g*
- *Protein: 1.5g*

Ingredients:

- *1 ½ cups all-purpose flour*
- *½ cup granulated sugar*

- 2 teaspoons baking powder
- ½ teaspoon salt
- ½ teaspoon ground cinnamon
- ¼ teaspoon ground nutmeg
- ½ cup milk
- 1 large egg
- 4 tablespoons unsalted butter, melted
- 1 teaspoon vanilla extract
- Vegetable oil, for frying

For Coating:

- ½ cup granulated sugar
- 1 teaspoon ground cinnamon

Directions:

1. **Preheat Oil:** In a deep fryer or heavy-bottomed pot, heat vegetable oil to 350°F (175°C).

2. **Prepare Dry Ingredients:** In a large bowl, whisk together flour, sugar, baking powder, salt, cinnamon, and nutmeg.

3. **Combine Wet Ingredients:** In a separate bowl, whisk together milk, egg, melted butter, and vanilla extract.

4. **Mix:** Pour the wet ingredients into the dry ingredients and stir until just combined. Be careful not to overmix; the batter should be slightly lumpy.

5. Form Dough Balls: Using a spoon or small cookie scoop, drop small balls of dough (about 1 tablespoon each) into the hot oil. Fry in batches to avoid overcrowding the pot.

6. Fry: Fry the dough balls for about 2-3 minutes, or until golden brown and cooked through, turning occasionally for even cooking.

7. Drain and Coat: Remove the donut holes from the oil using a slotted spoon and drain on paper towels briefly. While still warm, roll each donut hole in the cinnamon-sugar mixture until coated evenly.

8. Serve: Serve the cinnamon sugar donut holes warm and enjoy!

CHOCOLATE CHIP COOKIES

- ➢ *Serving Size: Makes about 24 cookies*

- ➢ *Prep Time: 15 minutes*

- ➢ *Cooking Time: 10-12 minutes*

Nutrition Info (per cookie):

- Calories: 150
- Total Fat: 8g

- *Saturated Fat: 4.5g*
- *Cholesterol: 20mg*
- *Sodium: 90mg*
- *Total Carbohydrates: 19g*
- *Dietary Fiber: 1g*
- *Sugars: 12g*
- *Protein: 2g*

Ingredients:

- *1 cup (2 sticks) unsalted butter, softened*
- *3/4 cup granulated sugar*
- *3/4 cup packed brown sugar*
- *2 large eggs*
- *1 teaspoon vanilla extract*
- *2 1/4 cups all-purpose flour*
- *1 teaspoon baking soda*
- *1/2 teaspoon salt*
- *2 cups semisweet chocolate chips*

Directions:

1. Preheat your oven to 350°F (175°C). Line baking sheets with parchment paper.

2. In a large mixing bowl, cream together the softened butter, granulated sugar, and brown sugar until smooth and creamy.

3. Beat in the eggs, one at a time, then stir in the vanilla extract.

4. In a separate bowl, combine the flour, baking soda, and salt. Gradually add this dry mixture to the wet ingredients, mixing until well combined.

5. Fold in the chocolate chips until evenly distributed throughout the cookie dough.

6. Using a cookie scoop or spoon, drop rounded tablespoons of dough onto the prepared baking sheets, leaving some space between each cookie for spreading.

7. Bake in the preheated oven for 10-12 minutes, or until the edges are lightly golden.

8. Allow the cookies to cool on the baking sheets for a few minutes before transferring them to a wire rack to cool completely.

9. Enjoy your homemade chocolate chip cookies with a glass of milk or your favorite hot beverage!

APPLE TURNOVERS

- ➢ *Serving Size: Makes 6 turnovers*

- ➢ *Prep Time: 20 minutes*

> ➤ *Cooking Time: 20 minutes*

Nutrition Information (per serving):

- *Calories: 280*
- *Total Fat: 16g*
- *Saturated Fat: 4.5g*
- *Cholesterol: 25mg*
- *Sodium: 150mg*
- *Total Carbohydrates: 31g*
- *Dietary Fiber: 2g*
- *Sugars: 13g*
- *Protein: 3g*

Ingredients:

- *2 large apples, peeled, cored, and diced*
- *2 tablespoons unsalted butter*
- *1/4 cup granulated sugar*
- *1 teaspoon ground cinnamon*
- *1/4 teaspoon ground nutmeg*
- *1 tablespoon lemon juice*
- *1 package (17.3 ounces) puff pastry sheets, thawed*
- *1 egg, beaten (for egg wash)*
- *Powdered sugar, for dusting (optional)*

Directions:

1. Preheat your oven to 375°F (190°C). Line a baking sheet with parchment paper.

2. In a skillet over medium heat, melt the butter. Add the diced apples, granulated sugar, cinnamon, nutmeg, and lemon juice. Cook, stirring occasionally, until the apples are tender, about 5-7 minutes. Remove from heat and let cool slightly.

3. On a lightly floured surface, unfold the puff pastry sheets. Cut each sheet into 3 equal squares, making a total of 6 squares.

4. Spoon the cooked apple mixture onto the center of each pastry square.

5. Fold each pastry square diagonally to form a triangle, enclosing the apple filling. Press the edges firmly to seal.

6. Place the turnovers on the prepared baking sheet. Brush the tops with the beaten egg wash.

7. Bake in the preheated oven for 18-20 minutes, or until the turnovers are golden brown and puffed up.

8. Remove from the oven and let cool slightly on the baking sheet before serving.

9. Optional: Dust with powdered sugar before serving for an extra touch of sweetness.

BERRY CRISP

- ➢ *Serving Size: 6 servings*

- ➢ *Prep Time: 15 minutes*

- ➢ *Cooking Time: 40 minutes*

Nutrition Info (per serving):

- *Calories: 290*
- *Total Fat: 13g*
- *Saturated Fat: 8g*
- *Cholesterol: 31mg*
- *Sodium: 107mg*
- *Total Carbohydrates: 42g*
- *Dietary Fiber: 5g*
- *Sugars: 24g*
- *Protein: 3g*

Ingredients:

- *4 cups mixed berries (such as strawberries, blueberries, raspberries, blackberries)*
- *1/4 cup granulated sugar*
- *1 tablespoon lemon juice*
- *1/2 teaspoon vanilla extract*
- *1 cup old-fashioned rolled oats*
- *1/2 cup all-purpose flour*
- *1/2 cup packed brown sugar*

- 1/2 teaspoon ground cinnamon
- 1/4 teaspoon salt
- 1/2 cup unsalted butter, cold and cut into small pieces

Directions:

1. Preheat your oven to 350°F (175°C). Grease a 9-inch baking dish.

2. In a large bowl, combine the mixed berries, granulated sugar, lemon juice, and vanilla extract. Toss gently to coat the berries evenly. Transfer the berry mixture into the prepared baking dish, spreading it out evenly.

3. In another bowl, mix together the oats, flour, brown sugar, cinnamon, and salt. Add the cold butter pieces and use your fingers or a pastry cutter to mix until the mixture resembles coarse crumbs.

4. Sprinkle the oat mixture evenly over the berries in the baking dish.

5. Bake in the preheated oven for 35 to 40 minutes, or until the topping is golden brown and the berry mixture is bubbling.

6. Remove from the oven and let it cool slightly before serving.

7. Serve warm, optionally with a scoop of vanilla ice cream or a dollop of whipped cream.

CHURROS WITH CHOCOLATE SAUCE

> ➤ **Serving Size: Makes about 12 churros**

> ➤ **Prep Time: 15 minutes**

> ➤ **Cooking Time: 15 minutes**

Nutrition Information (per serving):

- Calories: 235
- Total Fat: 13g
- Saturated Fat: 4g
- Cholesterol: 9mg
- Sodium: 127mg
- Total Carbohydrates: 30g
- Dietary Fiber: 1g
- Sugars: 15g
- Protein: 2g

Ingredients:

For the churros:

- 1 cup water
- 2 1/2 tablespoons white sugar
- 1/2 teaspoon salt
- 2 tablespoons vegetable oil
- 1 cup all-purpose flour
- 2 quarts oil for frying

- 1/2 cup white sugar, or to taste
- 1 teaspoon ground cinnamon

For the chocolate sauce:

- 1/2 cup heavy cream
- 1 cup semisweet chocolate chips
- 1/4 teaspoon vanilla extract

Directions:

1. In a small saucepan over medium heat, combine water, 2 1/2 tablespoons sugar, salt, and 2 tablespoons vegetable oil. Bring to a boil and remove from heat. Stir in flour until mixture forms a ball.

2. Heat oil for frying in deep-fryer or deep skillet to 375 degrees F (190 degrees C). Pipe strips of dough into hot oil using a pastry bag. Fry until golden; drain on paper towels.

3. Combine 1/2 cup sugar and cinnamon. Roll drained churros in cinnamon and sugar mixture.

4. For the chocolate sauce, heat the heavy cream in a small saucepan until it just begins to simmer. Remove from heat and stir in the chocolate chips until smooth. Stir in vanilla extract.

5. Serve churros warm with chocolate sauce for dipping.

PINEAPPLE UPSIDE-DOWN CAKE

- ➢ *Serving Size: 8 servings*

- ➢ *Prep Time: 20 minutes*

- ➢ *Cooking Time: 40-45 minutes*

Nutrition Info: (per serving)

- *Calories: 320*
- *Total Fat: 12g*
- *Saturated Fat: 7g*
- *Cholesterol: 65mg*
- *Sodium: 260mg*
- *Total Carbohydrates: 51g*
- *Dietary Fiber: 1g*
- *Sugars: 36g*
- *Protein: 3g*

Ingredients:

- *1/4 cup (60g) unsalted butter*
- *2/3 cup (130g) packed brown sugar*
- *1 can (20 oz) pineapple slices in juice, drained*
- *Maraschino cherries (optional)*
- *1 1/3 cups (170g) all-purpose flour*
- *1 cup (200g) granulated sugar*
- *1/3 cup (80ml) vegetable oil*
- *1 1/2 teaspoons baking powder*

- 1/2 teaspoon salt
- 2/3 cup (160ml) pineapple juice
- 2 large eggs

Directions:

1. Preheat your oven to 350°F (175°C). In a 9-inch round cake pan, melt the butter in the oven.

2. Sprinkle the brown sugar evenly over the melted butter. Arrange the pineapple slices in a single layer over the brown sugar. Place cherries in the center of each pineapple slice, if desired.

3. In a medium bowl, whisk together flour, granulated sugar, baking powder, and salt.

4. Add oil, pineapple juice, and eggs to the flour mixture. Beat with an electric mixer on low speed until combined, then beat on high speed for 2 minutes, scraping the bowl occasionally.

5. Pour the batter over the pineapple slices in the pan, spreading it evenly.

6. Bake for 40-45 minutes or until a toothpick inserted in the center comes out clean.

7. Immediately run a knife around the edge of the pan to loosen the cake. Place a serving plate upside down over the pan, then turn the plate and pan over. Leave the pan

over the cake for a few minutes to allow the topping to drizzle over the cake. Remove the pan and serve the cake warm or at room temperature.

Made in the USA
Las Vegas, NV
06 December 2024

13452073R00046